touched by a saint

CARDINAL BASIL HUME

SISTER NIRMALA

PRINCE PHILIP

CARDINAL JOHN O'CONNOR

HILLARY RODHAM CLINTON

EDWARD KENNEDY

ISMAIL MERCHANT

FR. ANDREW GREELEY

PRINCESS CAROLINE

SARAH FERGUSON

AND OTHERS

PERSONAL ENCOUNTERS WITH MOTHER TERESA

touched by a saint

SUSAN CRIMP

 SORIN BOOKS   Notre Dame, IN

All of the statements and testimonies in this book are used with the speaker's or writer's permission.

Cardinal George Basil Hume's homily at the Memorial Mass for Mother Teresa is used by permission of Westminster Cathedral, London. All rights reserved.

Prince Philip's speech at the presentation of the Templeton Prize to Mother Teresa is used by permission of Buckingham Palace, London. All rights reserved.

The interviews with Sister Nirmala and Cardinal John O'Connor were conducted by the author and are used with their permission.

International Standard Book Number: 1-893732-22-3

Library of Congress Card Number: 00-102080

Cover and text design by Katherine Robinson Coleman

Photography credits:

Susan Crimp: 20, 22, 25.

Associated Press Photos: Bikas Das 35; Saurabh Das 50, 53; Peter Dejong 48; Alexis Duclos 122; John Gress 120, Katsumi Kasahara 47; David Longstreath 31; Bebe Matthews 39; John Moore 45; Eric Risberg; Bock Staver 66; Mari Stringer 32, 42, 117; staff 112; White House 82.

Denver Rocky Mountain News: Glenn Asakawa 58.

Printed and bound in the United States of America.

This book is dedicated to

Mother Teresa

in grateful appreciation of the love

she showed the world.

Thank you.

Susan Crimp

"We can do no great things; only small things with great love."

MOTHER TERESA

What good is it, my brothers and sisters, if you say have faith but do not have works? Can faith save you? If a brother or sister is naked and lacks daily food, and one of you says to them, "Go in peace; keep warm and eat your fill," and yet you do not supply their bodily needs, what is the good of that? So faith by itself, if it has no works, is dead. . . . Show me your faith apart from your works, and I by my works will show you my faith.

JAMES 2:14-18

CONTENTS

ACKNOWLEDGMENTS

$\mathcal{M}$any people assisted me in one way or another with the preparation of this book which is compiled from a film I have made on Mother Teresa. First, the Missionaries of Charity allowed me into their many homes to film and see their love of Christ firsthand. Special thanks to Sister Nirmala who made this whole project possible and who took time out to be interviewed and provide tremendous insight into Mother Teresa. Thanks of the same magnitude must also be extended to Sister Priscilla who proved indispensable in ensuring accuracy in the factual data which I have gathered and who gave me time and tremendous encouragement throughout this project. I must also convey tremendous gratitude to Sister Dominga and Sister Sabita who provided great assistance to me. I am also eternally grateful to Sister Ann Therese whose guided tours of Calcutta gave me tremendous insight into Mother Teresa's impact on that city. Words will never convey how very grateful I am to each and every one of you. And to all the sisters and volunteers around the world who each and every day help the poorest of the poor.

I would also like to thank each person who provided testimony on Mother, especially Hillary Rodham Clinton, who was the first to say yes. I am grateful to the Archdiocese of New York, Cardinal O'Connor, Bishop Ahern, and Joseph Zwelling for all that they have done; Senator Edward Kennedy and his staff, especially Melody Miller; and to Buckingham Palace and Sarah Ferguson for their participation.

This project would also never have been completed without my production team who worked tirelessly to make Mother's name live on: Sam Somawru, my Director of Photography; my Producers Keira Brings, Susan Lawlor, Braden Twoomy, and Gary McCaffety. To each one of you, who gave so much of yourselves, I am extremely grateful. Words alone will also never express my utmost thanks to Cindy Adams who has done more for this project than anyone could ever imagine. Ironically for someone whose business it is to make headlines, Cindy does so much behind the scenes that most people will never know. For your sincerity of kindness, I thank you. Thanks also to Rev. Father W. Cleary.

I would also like to thank my own family, especially John Edward Crimp, Frederick, Shirley, and Steven Crimp, and various friends who have helped me in one way or another. Thanks also to Patrick McGeary, Marketing Director of Sorin Books, and Robert Hamma, Editorial Director, who took this book from conception to completion with love and grace. I also acknowledge with grateful thanks the work of the Associated Press, Reuters, New York Post, Westminster Cathedral, American Media, Catholic New York, and APA Publications whose work I have included in this book. I also write in memory of Sean Leddy, who did so much for Mother Teresa.

PREFACE

There are certain things a person will never forget in life. Meeting a saint is certainly one of them. I still remember vividly my own first meeting with Mother Teresa of Calcutta. I was teaching class to her contemplative sisters in the South Bronx. When I arrived that day the sisters told me they had a surprise for me. After class, as I was standing in the hallway, suddenly there was Mother Teresa. She walked over to me, and, putting a rosary (my most treasured possession) into my hand, she said to me, "Thank you for teaching my sisters!" I was overwhelmed, to say the least!

I was to meet Mother many more times. It was such a privilege! I considered Mother a good friend. Another experience I'll never forget happened after saying Mass for Mother and her sisters in Harlem. She came into the sacristy, and we talked for about half an hour. At one point, she reached into her pocket, took out a little card, and handed it to me. With a grin from ear to ear, she said to me, "Father, have one of my business cards!" But Mother's "business card" was not like any other I had ever seen—no address, phone, fax, or e-mail! It just stated Mother's business very simply:

The fruit of silence is prayer.
The fruit of prayer is faith.
The fruit of faith is love.
The fruit of love is service.
The fruit of service is peace!

Mother Teresa's "business card" summed up her life and was the secret for her great impact on the world. From her inner silence, prayer, and faith sprang an enormous love and generosity to serve, which brought inward and outward peace to individuals and communities alike. From humble beginnings, she was building what Pope John Paul II called "a civilization of love," or what she preferred to call "something beautiful for God."

We can be deeply grateful to Susan Crimp for her present book in which, with care and sensitivity, she preserves reminiscences of persons who had met Mother Teresa or were affected by the enormous labor of love of the remarkable woman many call "the saint of the gutters." This book will help assure that the memory and mission of Mother Teresa will ever remain a living treasure for the human family of all God's children.

FR. ANDREW APOSTOLI, CFR

INTRODUCTION

I am grateful that in my lifetime I met a saint. I am honored that she blessed me, and I also feel somewhat charmed that I shared the same birthday (August 26) with Mother Teresa. It is also fascinating to me that as a journalist, having met and chronicled the lives of so many well-known figures, including royalty, meeting this little woman would have the most profound effect on me. Mother Teresa was unique, possessing a presence that I had never witnessed before and sadly will not see again. Mother Teresa possessed a compassion beyond compare, a humanity that I have never seen in another human being, and an aura which was so outstanding that words cannot describe it. Mother Teresa is, I believe, a saint in heaven because she proved, by her total commitment to Jesus and the poor, that she was a living saint here on earth.

Unlike any other human being of the twentieth century, Mother Teresa was able to break down the barriers that usually separate all of us. She gained the respect of kings and queens, heads of state, captains of industry, the rich and famous, and most important, the poorest of the poor. Mother Teresa truly embraced the whole world, and in turn people from all creeds, classes, nationalities, races, and religions adored her.

The last time I saw Mother Teresa was in the Bronx. Ironically, she was with Princess Diana. Over the years I had covered every one of the princess's visits to America, and I had seen her at many glittering events and functions. On this occasion, however, she was by Mother Teresa's side with America's less financially fortunate. The rich spirituality of Mother Teresa made this moment one of the most memorable photo opportunities the world's press had ever seen.

Sadly, within a period of two months, both Mother and Diana would be gone. And while millions of words have been subsequently written about the late princess, comparatively few have been shared about Mother Teresa.

As a journalist I felt compelled to remember this remarkable woman and to travel the world and discover the lives she touched, and what people had to say about her. The following is a collection of anecdotes about Mother Teresa, from a wide range of people, some of whose lives were changed by meeting her, others who simply wanted to pay tribute to her.

Mother Teresa was a woman who spent a lifetime loving those the world had forgotten. May we, in preserving these memories of her, keep the spirit of this saint alive forever.

While none of us can save the whole world, Mother Teresa showed us that there is no excuse not to save a small part of it. For that small section of humanity that she helped directly—as well as all those who were touched by her grace, strength, and faith—the world was unquestionably made a better place.

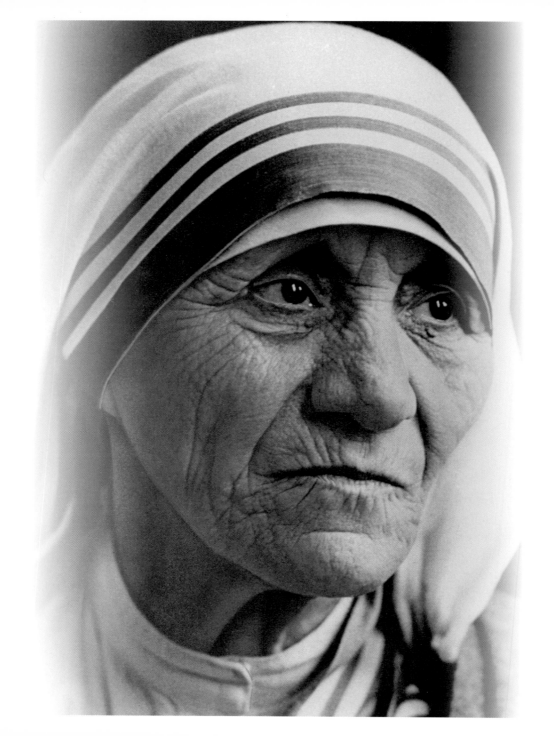

mother's life

Born Agnes Gonxha Bojaxhiu, Mother Teresa, as she would later be named, began life in Skopje, Yugoslavia, on August 26, 1910. She was the daughter of a prosperous Albanian businessman and the youngest of three children. By the time she was seven her father had died, causing a change in the family's economic circumstance. In later life Mother said very little about her childhood, but she did reveal that by the age of twelve, she had decided that she wanted to be a nun.

At the age of eighteen, she entered the order of The Sisters of Our Lady of Loreto in Ireland. Following her training in Dublin, she went to India in 1929 to teach geography at St. Mary's High School for girls in Calcutta. She took her final vows in 1937.

It was while she was working at St. Mary's that she was moved by the poverty of the destitute and dying who lay on the streets outside. One night on a train to a retreat in Darjeeling, she heard the call of God. "The message was clear," she said. "I was to leave the convent and help the poor while living among them." In 1948, after seeking permission and being told to wait a year, she was allowed by Pope Pius XII to leave her post at the convent and begin a ministry among the sick.

Mother Teresa and her associates were approved within the archdiocese of Calcutta as the Missionaries of Charity. She received three months of nursing training with the American

Medical Missionary Sisters and started living, as God had directed her, among the poorest of the poor.

Later the order was recognized as a pontifical congregation under the jurisdiction of Rome. Members of the congregation take four vows on acceptance by the religious community. In addition to the three religious vows taken—poverty, chastity, and obedience—is a fourth vow pledging wholehearted, free service to the poorest of the poor, whom Mother Teresa described as the embodiment of Christ.

In 1952 Mother opened Nirmal Hriday (pure heart), a home for the dying. A year later an orphanage followed. In 1962 Mother Teresa won the first of her many awards for humanitarian work—the Indian government gave her the Padna Shri (Magnificent Lotus) award for "distinguished service." Over the years Mother would use the money from such prizes to found hundreds of homes.

In 1963 there was a new branch to the Order, the Missionary Brothers of Charity. As her work continued, Mother Teresa reached out to those in need around the world, providing comfortable and dignified places for the dying, schools for street children, and food centers for those in need. Mother Teresa's ability to achieve the impossible grew with her order.

In 1979 she received the Nobel Peace Prize, and in 1982 she even managed to persuade the Israelis and Lebanese to stop shooting long enough to rescue thirty-seven retarded children from a hospital in besieged Beirut.

Today Mother's Missionaries of Charity can be found throughout the world serving those in need, from Iraq to Iceland, from Manhattan to Milan. Indeed, by the time you have finished reading this book, the Missionaries of Charity will have helped thousands more dying, starving, and helpless adults and children in every area of the world.

Each day these remarkable women and men help those in need, love those shunned by the rest of society. They do it for Jesus, but let us never forget that this entire global devotion was made possible by the grace of God and Mother Teresa.

The more humble a man is and the more subject to God, the wiser he will be in all things, and the more at peace.

THE IMITATION OF CHRIST

CALCUTTA, INDIA

Calcutta has been called many things: "The most wicked place in the universe" according to one visitor. A city where cholera and the cyclones come and go in turn, a city "by the sewerage rendered fetid, by the sewer made impure," wrote Rudyard Kipling. Winston Churchill once confided, "I shall always be glad to have seen it for the reason that it will be unnecessary for me to see it again." Indeed many negative descriptions have been made about this fascinating city.

Yet while there is extreme poverty and a certain amount of chaos, this place was not also called "city of joy" without reason. Despite the poverty, the people of Calcutta display happiness, and it remains India's warmest city and the country's intellectual capital. There are still traces of the fact that Calcutta was once a city of palaces, and that Lord Wellesley set a trend when he built Government House on the grounds that "India is a country of splendor, of extravagance and of outward appearances."

Calcutta was the grandest city ever built by Europeans outside of Europe. As one traveler in the eighteenth century described, "We felt we were approaching a great capital. On landing, I was struck with the general appearance of grandeur in all the buildings."

Economically, the days of grandeur have long gone, though it is not hard to imagine the splendor that used to surround Calcutta. At the height of its glory in the nineteenth century, Calcutta was called the second city of the British empire, rivaling London in its riches and social refinement.

That was then. Unfortunately things are different in Calcutta today. The city's decline started in 1911, when the capital of British India was moved to Delhi, just north of the present capital, New Delhi. Calcutta had to make way for more people with the 1947 partition that ended British colonial rule, making an independent India and Pakistan and creating a flow of refugees across the newly created borders.

Things grew worse in the wake of the Bangladesh war in 1971, and another population surge overburdened the city and urban services which have been on the verge of collapse ever since.

Today Calcutta is home to the poorest of the world's poor. It is a place to break Western hearts. Many who visit from abroad see it only as a desperate place for destitute people, while others are inspired to learn from the people here, to understand how and why they seem so happy against such a horrible backdrop. Indeed many Westerners can learn a lot from the people's ability to accept and embrace Calcutta as their home. As Mother Teresa once said, "The poor are very great people, they can teach us many beautiful things."

Physically the city is attached like an ear to the banks of the Hooghly River. The inner ear is the "White Town," the former European city of spacious homes and broad avenues. Beyond that, encompassing the villages, lies the native section

or "Black Town," of narrow lanes, slums, bazaars, temples, mansions, and warehouses.

Probably most shocking to the Western eye is the harsh day-to-day reality of Calcutta. Everywhere, people sleep on the ground, many with nothing to shield them from the hard concrete or dark cold. The smell of steamy, pungent trash heaped at the sides of the streets is smothering.

The homeless—and the streets are lined with them—cook in the streets. Rice and scraps of food simmer in tin pots resting on overturned square steel containers with wood burning underneath.

People sell vegetables. Hot tea is served in leaves twisted into cones. Lining the streets are small shops where nearly everything is sold, from tourism services to T-shirts to Campa-Cola—India's version of Coca-Cola. The same scenes are repeated hundreds of times throughout Calcutta. Along the Hooghly River, people cook and sleep, and they bathe and wash clothes in dirty water.

Men wear red and white checkered cloth wrapped around their waists and nearly reaching their ankles. Women dress in brightly colored saris. Their bathroom is the fire hydrant on the street. At the break of each new day, they rise from their pavement and gather. Those who do not rise have died of starvation or disease during the night.

On every road, young women with dirt-smeared faces and outstretched arms loosely holding naked babies beg to anyone who walks by. Some children are deliberately deformed so the beggars can get more money. This is Calcutta—a place that no one would want to call home, unless they had the patience of a saint, unless they were Mother Teresa.

The poor are very great people,
they can teach us many beautiful things.

MOTHER TERESA

mother's death

*I*n a world mourning the loss of Princess Diana, I first learned of Mother Teresa's death via an Associated Press advisory. It stated quite simply, "Mother Teresa dead."

The following morning tributes from the world's press began.

SEPTEMBER 6, 1997

Mother Teresa Mourned by the World

Mother Teresa—the tiny "saint of the gutters" whose untiring ministry to the poor and terminally ill made her synonymous with charity—died yesterday of a massive heart attack.

The Nobel Peace Prize-winning nun, in declining health for the past eight years, was eighty-seven when she collapsed at her Missionaries of Charity convent in Calcutta—five days after the tragic death of her friend Princess Diana. "Her heart, which held up for all those years, suddenly gave way," said Dr. Vincenzo Bilotta, her physician in Rome.

A boy, name unknown, waits in line out-side St. Thomas' church with a bouquet of flowers, to pay his respects to Mother Teresa in Calcutta.

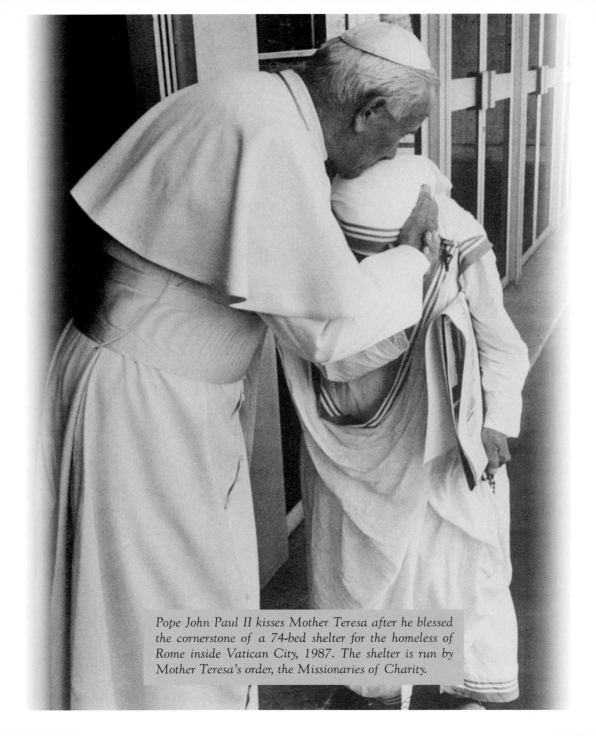

Pope John Paul II kisses Mother Teresa after he blessed the cornerstone of a 74-bed shelter for the homeless of Rome inside Vatican City, 1987. The shelter is run by Mother Teresa's order, the Missionaries of Charity.

For half a century, Mother Teresa comforted the destitute, sheltered abandoned babies, cared for lepers, comforted the mentally ill—and became one of the world's most powerful voices, arguing against abortion, contraception, and divorce.

Accolades poured in from secular and religious leaders.

Pope John Paul II was "deeply moved and pained" by the death "because he was very close to this sister who dedicated her life to helping people in the world who were the poorest, the most neglected and the abandoned," said the Vatican's deputy spokesperson, Father Ciro Benedettini.

President Clinton called Mother Teresa "an incredible person," and the U.S. House of Representatives observed a moment of silence in her memory.

The chairman of the Nobel Peace Prize awards committee, Francis Sejersted, said the beloved nun was a symbol of humanitarianism. "Hers is one of the awards we look back on with great joy and satisfaction," he said.

For most, Mother Teresa's energy and dedication were matched only by her humility. To all, she was identifiable for her diminutive stature, kindly smile, and plain, white sari with three blue bands. Those three bands represented her life of faith, hope, and charity.

"To meet her is to feel utterly humble," Prime Minister Indira Gandhi once remarked. Indeed there was no one quite like Mother Teresa.

She's taken her place among God's greatest heroes.

At a pit stop in Charleston, South Carolina, a few years ago, Mother Teresa was asked at a press conference about the popular notion she was a saint.

"Please," she laughed. "Let me die first."

Yesterday, it happened. In the slum-ridden city of Calcutta, where she pursued her epic life of love and charity, Mother Teresa's generous heart—great and strong—finally gave out. Now the whole world can answer the question.

She truly was a saint, a woman of incomparable beauty and virtue, who served God by serving the poorest people on earth. The crippled and the blind, the starving and the deserted, the lame and the leprous—she embraced them all, fed them, begged for them, scrubbed them, loved them, and buried them.

Mother Teresa was, by my biased light, the woman of the twentieth century, a towering figure of humility and holiness, devoid of cant and overflowing with genuine compassion. She did it all not for human respect or personal aggrandizement, but out of love for God.

What never ceased to amaze me about Mother Teresa was her unwavering public stand against the degradations of modern culture, while at the same time winning the hearts of everyone from kings and presidents to waifs and orphans. They loved her in the gutters and they recognized her in the palace of Nobel Prizes.

Catholic or Jew, Protestant or Moslem, Hindu or agnostic—all saw the goodness and spirituality shining out of her small, tough little body. In a world devoted to materialism, ambition, and ostentation, she chose poverty, frugality, and service. In the celebrity era of the rich, famous, and powerful, she sought the outcast, the anonymous. In the world of instant gratification, she practiced self-denial.

Millions may have loved Mother Teresa, but I'm not sure they all understood her. It is eerie that her death should come in the midst of great global outpouring of sorrow over the loss of Princess Diana. Their worlds were polar opposites, their lives as different as night and day, yet they shared a common bond of sympathy for the dispossessed.

Mother Teresa once said: "The greatest disease in the world today is not leprosy or tuberculosis, but the feeling of being unwanted, uncared for, unloved."

The differences between these two women are as sharp in death as in life. Diana continues to be mourned even today, a tragic figure, taken too soon at thirty-six in the bloom of life. Mother Teresa's passing at eighty-seven did not plunge the world into deep sadness, grief, and anger. Rather, it was more of a celebration, a joyful recognition of a long life of hard work, strict discipline, amazing accomplishments, outstanding sanctity, remarkable sacrifice, and overwhelming love.

Malcolm Muggeridge, the late British broadcaster whose TV documentary and book on Mother Teresa propelled her into the world spotlight, said of her: "To choose as Mother Teresa did, to live in the slums of Calcutta, amidst all the dirt and disease and misery, signified a spirit so indomitable, a faith so intractable, a love so abounding, that I felt abashed."

The whole world felt the same way about her.

Mother Teresa knew all about death. In her lifetime, she took in more than one hundred thousand broken human beings, unloved, unwanted. Many died in her tender arms.

She said: "Death is the most decisive moment in human life. It is like a coronation, to die in peace with God. I have never seen anyone die desperate or blaspheming. They all die serenely, almost with joy."

She told of one man she rescued from the streets and took to her home for dying destitutes. "He said to me, 'I have lived like an animal in the streets, but I am going home to die like an angel.'"

Yesterday, the beloved Mother Teresa, after years of poor health, met her maker, the one she served all her life. We can only guess how that meeting went, but one thing is for sure— the choirs of angels would be in high voice to greet her for her "coronation."

WESTMINSTER CATHEDRAL, LONDON, ENGLAND

MEMORIAL HOMILY BY

CARDINAL GEORGE BASIL HUME, OSB

*G*od speaks to us through events and persons. Twelve days ago, I think he used Diana to make us pause and reflect, to ask questions about life and death, their meaning and purpose. Now through Mother Teresa, he is drawing our attention, surely to the answers: the primacy of God, the true meaning of love, and the value of every human life.

Why was this nun able to achieve so much and make such an impact on the world? Mother Teresa followed Christ with simplicity and passionate conviction. Behind the ceaseless activity lay hours of silence, prayer, and rapt adoration.

She never swerved from the religious observances in which she had been formed as a young nun both in Ireland and India. Her energy flowed from hunger, a life of prayer, from the liturgy and sacraments of the church. And through daily faithfulness she came gradually to personify the twin commandments that lie at the heart of Christian life. She always had before her eyes the command to love the Lord God with her whole self and all her energies and to love her neighbor as herself.

Mother Teresa says goodbye to Princess Diana after receiving a visit from her in 1997 in New York.

Mother Teresa acknowledges the audience's applause while addressing some 3,000 people at the San Jose Civic Auditorium, 1986.

What made her so special was the radical and total way she lived out those familiar ideals. She loved and served humanity because she had given herself without reserve to the love and service of God. She saw no distinction or conflict here: all was united in a single vision and an unconditional response.

This century has witnessed two world wars, immense slaughter, ruthless genocide, and the unique bestiality of the Holocaust. While many now enjoy unprecedented prosperity, some millions still die of hunger, deprivation, and disease throughout the developing world. Medical science helps us to ease, heal, and prolong human life, but, at the same time, millions of unborn lives are condemned to death by abortion and our society feels free to experiment on human embryos in the name of progress. Life in many aspects has become disposable and cheap.

Mother Teresa would have none of that. For her, each individual was an image of God to be cherished, respected, and served. She would rescue abandoned babies from trash cans in Calcutta. She would try to give homeless derelicts a roof over their heads and an experience, however fleeting, of Christian compassion and love before they died. She campaigned tirelessly for the right to life and against the spread of abortion. At all times and in every circumstance she stood for basic and positive values.

But another voice has been whispering these last days. Would it not have been better to spend more of the money she received on building new hospitals? Maybe. Should she have met and received money from those whom the rest of us

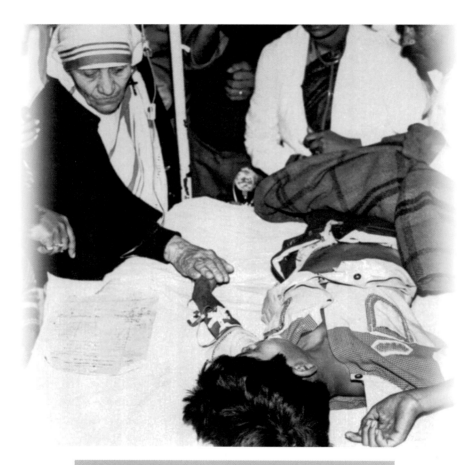

Mother Teresa comforts a young victim of the Bhopal gas disaster in Bhopal, India, 1984.

might shun? I do not know. Did she show more concern for compassion than for long-term development? I cannot tell. All I know is that love takes many forms, those inspired by it act in many different ways. But there is, however, a language of love which defies human wisdom.

Prudence has a role to play in our human affairs, no doubt. Yes, we must build hospitals. Yes, we must work for long-term development. But love can sometimes be reckless. Then it will jolt the rest of us out of our complacency, shame us to take action ourselves, upset, perhaps, our innate selfishness. Mother Teresa's commitment showed us the way. Her loving service knew no limits. To see her cradle an abandoned scrap of humanity in her arms was to see love in action. People who crowded round her often simply wanted to touch her. It was as if they could be healed by the energy of love that flowed from her. She went without question wherever there was human suffering and need. Her sisters are to be found now in over a hundred countries. Love like hers knows no boundaries, no prejudices, no limits.

God has spoken through recent events and persons. He has told us about the importance of compassion, understanding, and kindness. He has drawn our attention to the value of all human life and to the ways of loving service. Shall we listen to his voice and heed his prompting, or shall we not? It would be sad if we do not, wonderful if we do. Thank you, Mother Teresa, for what you did and what you are. Do I go now to pray for you? I am not so sure. I shall, however, be asking you to intercede for me, and the rest of us as well.

SEPTEMBER 13, 1997 — CALCUTTA, INDIA

World Cradles Mother to Sleep

Mother Teresa returned home today never to leave it again. On a gray September afternoon, eight Army officers bore her open coffin into Mother House after the poor and sick lined the streets and presidents and royalty gathered in the exclusive environs of a stadium to snatch a last glimpse.

*L*ike the slow march of the pallbearers, the city took its time to react to the loss of Mother Teresa of Calcutta, its outpouring of grief brimming over on the last day. A hushed silence descended on the thousands who had collected before an out-of-bounds Mother House as she was brought in after a journey that began in bright sunshine at St. Thomas Church. The gun salute which brought the curtains down on the pomp of a state funeral was muted by the silent tears of the mourners who braved the unkind weather to bid her farewell. People thronged St. Thomas's church from 6 in the morning. At 8:30 a.m., eight Army officers emerged from the church with the coffin on their shoulders.

Officers and jawans slow-marched 50 meters and placed the coffin on the gun carriage, the same carriage that carried

The people she loved mourn the loss of Mother Teresa, September 1997.

Mahatma Gandhi and Phandit Jawaharial Nehru to their funerals. The cortege, followed by a convoy of sixteen vehicles, carrying army top brass and nuns of the Missionaries of Charity, entered Park Street, the city's heart. It was somber and numb. On a day of high emotion, reactions were muted, but heartfelt. Thousands upon thousands stood on a five-kilometer route to Netaji Indoor Stadium. Some wept openly. Some shed a silent tear. And some merely held their palms to the sky, crossed themselves, and showered petals on the cortege.

As the cortege entered Jawaharial Nehru Road, there was a sudden burst of emotion. Mourners broke through the barricade and ran toward the convoy. The police had to drive them back and resort to lathicharge. The gun carriage rolled along, towed by a field tractor laden with flowers and wreaths, past Victoria Memorial and into Red Road.

At 10 a.m., a distant drum and a funeral note was heard inside Netaji Indoor Stadium. The band playing the Death March entered. Then came Mother Teresa on the shoulders of the pallbearers. The 12,000-strong congregation rose to its feet.

Among them, queens and first ladies, presidents and prime ministers, former heads of state, ministers, and envoys from all the continents. Yes, representatives of fifty countries, about half of them from the developed world, gathered, standing alongside representatives of poor nations, to say goodbye to Mother.

46

*Indian soldiers carry Mother Teresa's coffin past India's
Sonia Gandhi, widow of former Prime Minister Rajiv
Gandhi, center, Aline Chretien of Canada, second left,
and U.S. first lady Hillary Rodham Clinton at the start
of Mother Teresa's funeral Mass in the Netaji Indoor
Stadium in Calcutta, Sept. 13, 1997.*

Cardinal Angelo Sodano, Vatican's Secretary of State, blesses Mother Teresa with incense during her funeral Mass in the Netaji Indoor Stadium in Calcutta, 1997. Mother Teresa was later taken to the motherhouse for burial.

The gates of the stadium were not so wide open for the poorest of the poor to pay their last respects to their Mother, but they were there in the thousands lining the route of the funeral procession, waiting patiently for the last glimpse.

The funeral services were led by Cardinal A. Sodano, the Vatican's secretary of state and the pope's representative.

And so the world had come to Calcutta, a place that without Mother Teresa may have been forgotten. It was a fitting finale, as the poorest of the poor cried along with the richest of the world's rich. It was a funeral fit for a saint and touched everyone who saw it. Just as Mother Teresa had done in life, so too in death did she embrace all people. As an indication of the diversity of the people who loved Mother Teresa, later that day, as beggars cried in the streets, Her Royal Highness Queen Noor of Jordan drove to the airport with tears streaming down her face. Like everyone else in Calcutta that day, Her Royal Highness knew, as did the rest of the world, that the kindest woman to grace our lifetime was gone, and that we might never see anyone quite so kind on this earth again. All we can do now is thank God that she was here at all and pray for her Missionaries of Charity throughout the world.

remembering mother

SISTER NIRMALA

CALCUTTA, INDIA

Having seen how the world was remembering Mother, I went in search of other memories. My journey to remember Mother Teresa began in India where I would meet her successor, Sister Nirmala.

When Mother Teresa died, the task of running the Missionaries of Charity—the order Mother started—fell to Sister Nirmala. The community had elected Sister Nirmala to the leadership of the order prior to Mother's death. The new superior general has been described as a compassionate "carbon copy" of their revered foundress.

Sister Nirmala's life makes fascinating reading. Born into a Hindu family, this petite four-foot-ten-inch nun made her Christian conversion when she was seventeen and joined the Missionaries of Charity three months later. Upon realizing Sister Nirmala's academic excellence, Mother Teresa sent her to law school, and when she graduated she became the Missionaries' legal counsel.

Today it is Sister Nirmala's job to lead the community, an order comprising approximately five thousand sisters. There are some 450 brothers in a separate men's order. Their work is global, reaching out to 569 missions spread across 120

Mother Teresa blesses her successor Sister Nirmala during a news conference in Calcutta on March 14, 1997.

nations. In addition, there is an order of priests. The Missionaries of Charity rely solely upon donations for their survival. Their aim is to serve the poorest of the poor. They operate workshops for the unemployed, food centers, orphanages, leprosy centers, educational programs, and refuges for the mentally ill and aged. When I sat down to discuss Mother Teresa with Sister Nirmala at the order's headquarters in Calcutta, she still clearly missed her spiritual leader.

AN INTERVIEW WITH SISTER NIRMALA

Knowing Mother Teresa as well as you did, how would you describe her?

She was very human, very honest, and very faithful. Mother never wanted to be different or special, but she had a wonderful sense of humor.

When Mother was sick, she said she remembered one of her dreams. In the dream she died and went to heaven and Saint Peter said she couldn't come in because there were no poor people inside.

As she got sicker and sicker, I said to her, "What will you do if Saint Peter says the same thing again?" She said, "I will not leave. I know the Virgin Mary will come out and say to him. 'Please let her in, she's been so nice to me and has prayed to me every day of her life.'" Mother's sense of humor was like a child's, and it was so nice for us.

She hoped that people all over the world would receive tremendous joy in helping the poor, because in helping the poor, they would be helping God and that would bring so much peace and joy into their hearts. And that was not only for their time on earth, but also forevermore. What we do is very little. Our job is to make people aware of the poor and what some people have while others do not, to make people aware of the gifts they have and to give, and to give until it hurts—not from their surplus, but until it hurts.

How did you become aware of Mother Teresa's mission?

I spoke to a Catholic priest about my plans to become a nun and he told me about Mother Teresa. I was going to help my people in Nepal, but upon hearing him, instead of continuing with my plans I went to Mother. I went to visit her twice, but when I went again I was not going home. I remember I walked in and Mother Teresa had been working hard, as usual, and her hands were all black. I asked her for a blessing and she blessed me with her black hands—my face was all black. Because I had been there twice before and each time Mother had taken me to the train station, I told her, "Mother, this time I don't have to go home." She said, "Now you will go back from our house only in your coffin."

Can you describe the work that Mother Teresa started? What is a typical day here at the motherhouse and what other work did she initiate here in Calcutta?

The motherhouse on Bose Road in Calcutta is the central house of our society where 250 of us live. We get up at 4:40 a.m. and at 5:00 a.m. we pray. At 6:00 a.m. we have holy Mass and then we clean the house before 8:00 a.m., when we pray again. Then some of the sisters go out and work on the streets or go to our other houses in Calcutta.

We also have Mother Teresa's tomb here, which is open to the public, and we have lots of visitors. At noon we have lunch and prayers, then some of the sisters go back out on the streets and work. Between 6:00 p.m. and 7:00 p.m. we have adoration. Dinner is at 7:30 and then we pray again. We then have recreation for half an hour before 10:00 p.m., when we are all quite tired and we go to bed.

There are five other houses: Shisju Bhavan, which is the house for the children; Kalighat, the home for the destitute and dying; Prem Dan, the house for the mentally and physically handicapped; Tengra, for those who have problems and have been in prison; and Gandhiji Prem Nivas, the leprosy center.

Without the Missionaries of Charity, where would the people of Calcutta be?

I don't know. Many of them are from the street, and those that are not taken to hospital come to us. If we were not here, maybe the Lord would find some other way. He called Mother to serve the poorest of the poor, and he called her when she was here in Calcutta.

Mother Teresa won the respect of world leaders and many celebrities. One of the most famous friendships she shared was with Diana, Princess of Wales. What was the bond between them?

Their relationship was a beautiful one. They had the same goal: serving the poorest of the poor. Diana had tremendous love and respect for Mother, and Mother had love and respect for Diana—as I do too. I was not in India when Diana came here, but I met her with Mother in London and New York. When Diana died, Mother Teresa was very sad. Mother was sick that whole week. She spoke often about Diana at that time. There was to be a special Mass for Diana on Saturday, but on Friday Mother died.

I was with her on Thursday night. She was not well, and she did not come to chapel. On Friday she came to Mass and she had dinner, but she had a pan in the back and wasn't well at all. Then she went to bed and started to have this terrible cough. The doctor called me in and said that Mother was gone. I went to the chapel, where the novices were, and I told them, "Mother has gone home to Jesus," and all at once they let out this cry. It was quite incredible.

How should we remember Mother Teresa?

By keeping her spirit alive and putting into our lives what she started: love God and humanity, especially the poorest of the poor.

GILBERT ORTIZ

CHEYENNE, WYOMING

---

*On the saddest day of my life, she had given me
happiness and strength.*

*A thank-you note which Mother Teresa wrote to Ortiz back
in 1981 but forgot to mail finally arrived sixteen years later.
And from Gilbert Ortiz's point of view, it couldn't have come
at a better time.*

*It was March 1998, seven months after Mother Teresa's
death, that the letter arrived, accompanied by a cover letter
from Sister Nirmala, explaining how and why the letter was
never mailed.*

It was March 15, 1998, and I went to see my doctor, a kidney specialist. He showed me the MRI and told me that I had an aneurysm on my aorta that was one inch all the way around. He also told me that my kidneys were failing. I was terrified. I went home and explained everything the doctor had told me to my wife, and I told her not to tell my children. I then just went and sat down on the sofa and was very depressed.

My wife went off to the mailbox and she came back and said, "There's a letter here from the Missionaries of Charity."

I didn't quite register what the name meant, I thought it was just another charity maybe wanting a donation. At that time my mind was elsewhere. Then I opened the letter and I couldn't believe it; I thought I would go through the roof. There in front of me was a letter from Mother Teresa. She had been dead for seven months!

Now, I'm only five-foot-five, but at that moment I felt ten feet high. My favorite saint was Saint Thérèse and I had prayed to her every day, but Mother Teresa had performed a miracle for me. On the saddest day of my life, she had given me happiness and strength. I now pray to Mother every day, and I wear the medal they sent me around my neck. I feel at peace and my aneurysm has stopped growing; I feel healthier and I will begin dialysis in a year. Because of Mother Teresa I feel blessed and at peace. She couldn't have come into my life at a better time. I get chills thinking about it, but it was truly a miracle.

Every day some miracle happens.

MOTHER TERESA

MICHAEL   WAYNE   HUNTER

SAN   QUENTIN   PRISON

Incredible vitality and warmth came from her piercing eyes.

*I*n the summer of 1987, I had just finished my third year on San Quentin's death row, warehoused on the old death row, or "the shelf" as we call it.

On this particular day, I came into the tier at 8:30 a.m. on my way to work out with my friend Bob Harris. After lifting weights for a while, I was off to my cell to change into gym shorts to play basketball.

As I sat there on the tier, double-tying my shoes, the guard came down the gun-rail and asked what I was doing. "What does it look like?" I asked him.

"You're going to miss Mother Teresa," the guard said. "She's coming today."

I looked at him with a cynical smile. "You cops will do anything to keep from running us to the yard, won't you?" I said. "I'm not missing my sunshine. If she shows up, tell her to lace up some high-tops and meet me on the roof. I can post her up to the hoop, probably, and shoot over the top of her."

"Okay," the guard said. "But don't say I didn't warn you." Then he turned and walked away.

Whereupon a couple of alarm bells went off in my head. The guard, I told myself, had given up too easily. Maybe Mother Teresa was coming. Then I thought "Get real, Hunter." And I finished getting ready to rock, heading up to the roof with everyone else. But afterward, walking down the stairs back inside, I heard the guard on the gun-rail call. "Don't go into your cells and lock up. Mother Teresa stayed to see you guys too."

So I jogged up to the front in gym shorts and a tattered basketball shirt with the arms ripped out, and on the other side of the security screen was this tiny woman who looked one hundred years old. Yes, it was Mother Teresa.

You have to understand that, basically, I'm a dead man. I don't have to observe any sort of social convention. As a result, I can break all the rules, say what I want. But one look at this Nobel Prize winner, this woman so many view as a living saint, and I was speechless.

Incredible vitality and warmth came from her piercing eyes. She smiled at me, blessed a religious medal, and handed it to me. I wouldn't have walked voluntarily to the front of the tier to see the warden, the governor, or the president. I could not care less about them. But standing before this woman, all I could say was, "Thank you, Mother Teresa."

Then I stepped back to let another dead man come forward to receive his medal. As I stood there looking at the medal, I knew my wife was going to treasure it. After all, in her youth, she [had] seriously consider[ed] becoming a nun. It occurred to me that her sister was going to be absolutely jealous. Perhaps, I thought, I should try to get a second medal.

Taking a chance, I walked the few steps back and asked Mother Teresa for my sister-in-law. She smiled, blessed one, and handed it to me. Once again, the warmth of her presence surrounded me. Then Mother Teresa turned and pointed her hand at the sergeant on the shelf. "What you do to these men," she told him, "you do to God." The sergeant almost faded away in surprise and wonder.

Then out came the camera, and some guards began taking pictures of themselves with Mother Teresa. I was surprised by how professionally she posed. Then it occurred to me that she was used to doing this with some of the most powerful people in the world.

That night, as I wrote my wife and sister-in-law and sent their medals, I told them how I couldn't help reflecting on how this woman had chosen to live her life and what she had accomplished, and how I, in contrast, had just thrown my life away. It was a humbling experience.

So Mother Teresa came and went. The sergeant was affected by her words for a whole day and a half.

My wife who is also named Teresa (though I call her Terri) started wearing the medal on a chain around her neck. It became one of her prized possessions. As time went by, however, I forgot how powerful I had found Mother Teresa's presence. Usually, in talking about her visit, I would just joke that she kept the Sarge at bay for thirty-six hours.

Then in 1989, my fifth year on death row, my wife told me that she couldn't remain married any longer. It was one of the toughest experiences of my life, right up there with when my mother died. Terri told me that she still loved me, but being married to a dead man was just too difficult. We divorced shortly after my death penalty appeal was rejected by the California Supreme Court. I was at my lowest ebb emotionally. This was when I began to recall the strength and warmth I had felt in Mother Teresa's presence.

I wrote to Terri and asked if I could borrow the medal that Mother had blessed for me. The medal would be hers, of course. I just wanted to borrow it to recapture some strength from that remarkable woman. I would return the medal when I left death row, probably upon my execution.

VERWELL CHAITTENDON

WARDEN, SAN QUENTIN

Mother Teresa's visit here had the most profound effect on the inmates. She was so small, but from her hands you could see how hard she had worked her whole life. Nobody here will ever forget the visit, it was one of the best days this prison has ever seen.

> *I believe in person-to-person. Every person is Christ for me, and since there is only one Jesus, that person is the one person in the world at that moment.*
>
> MOTHER TERESA

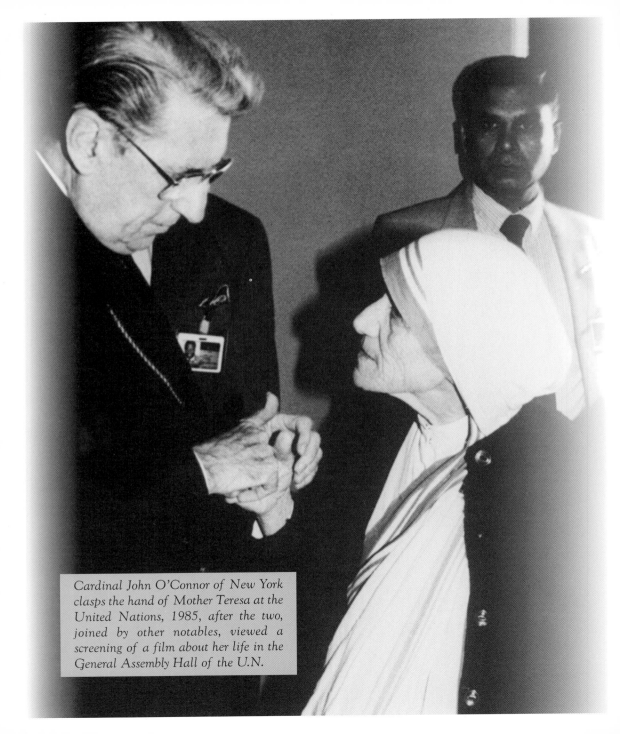

Cardinal John O'Connor of New York clasps the hand of Mother Teresa at the United Nations, 1985, after the two, joined by other notables, viewed a screening of a film about her life in the General Assembly Hall of the U.N.

AN INTERVIEW WITH

CARDINAL JOHN O'CONNOR

ARCHBISHOP OF NEW YORK

The first time she said to me,
"Give God permission," it changed my life.

Can you take us back to the time when you first met Mother Teresa?

The first time she said to me, "Give God permission," it changed my life. I had just been ordained a bishop and it was the last thing in the world I thought would happen to me, the last thing I wanted to happen to me. Leaving military service after twenty-seven years en route to my own archdiocese, thinking I was going to become a simple parish priest in a country parish with no debt, and then suddenly I'm called to Rome not only to be ordained a bishop, but a bishop for the armed forces. And it was then that Mother Teresa looked into me, through me, looked me up and down, and said, "Give God permission." I'd never heard that said before; it was obvious what she intended: God wants to reach out to others through your hands, he wants to speak to others through your lips, and God wants others to look into your eyes and see him. . . use you as an instrument in other words. So that really has determined these nineteen plus years of my life.

What made Mother Teresa different from other spiritual leaders?

I think perhaps in part because she was so convinced that she wasn't different. I think that most of the time she was astonished that there was so much fuss made about her.

We became very close. I apparently was able to say things to her that I'm sure other people could have said, but they didn't think they could. I would kid her, seem to ridicule her, and she would laugh and laugh and laugh. Which made me think that she thought that I was seeing the real Mother Teresa, and that everybody else in the world was fooled. That wasn't true at all.

She was the essence of holiness herself. Her humility was truly extraordinary. I think sometimes that humility wasn't captured because people thought this was an act. It's a strange act to live that way; to sleep on the floor, in frighteningly crowded conditions, and to have absolutely no privacy, to eat almost nothing. You'd have to be almost psychotic, I think, to want to do that intentionally, maybe for a day, a half-hour, but it was every day and every night, it was constant with her and there was not a splinter of fraudulency in her being.

How does it make you feel when people say no one could be that good?

I think one of the reasons is many of us who might make such allegations would make them because we can't imagine ourselves becoming anything like that. So we assume that nobody else could do it. And I think some of the accusations have been prompted by pure hatred of goodness itself. We do really, because of original sin or whatever the other perversity that prompts it, we seem to take great delight in destroying anything that seems good and whole, after all, people go to museums and slash through beautiful paintings, others take hammers, as someone did in St. Peter's, in Rome.

I think it's part of a perversity of humanity that just can't stand goodness. The Holy Father calls this a culture of death. I think it is a culture of death, not only because we put unborn babies to death and now we have physician-assisted suicide, but life, goodness, and beauty as God intended are one, and the culture of death just can't stand this and wants to attack it. Mother Teresa epitomized the ultimate in simplicity, the ultimate in honesty. Then there are some who simply didn't understand, when she would say hello to or accept money from some people.

As far as Mother Teresa was concerned, she always did what Christ would do. Christ was ridiculed, considered to be stupid and very foolish, because he would sit with drunkards, with prostitutes. He would have dinner with them, he let a woman come in and break a container of very, very precious ointment, which in those days could have been sold for a fortune, simply to wash his feet with. It was Judas, the traitor, who said this ointment could be sold and the money given to the poor, but the funny thing is that Judas was the thief, this was the thief that sold Christ for thirty pieces of silver. So I think it's a lack of understanding, plus the fact that those who wanted to give Mother Teresa money, which she accepted for the poor, I think she recognized that they were trying in some way to compensate for what they had done, for the dishonesties. Looking at it objectively, is it better that they would die with everything they stole, or give half of it away to the poor?

In that sense I think she was very pragmatic and it helped their consciences. I don't think she was ever concerned about enhancing their image or having her own image in anyway soiled. She did what she did. I remember her coming here one Christmas Eve and she had already contacted the governor and after she contacted the governor, she contacted the mayor, and then she came to see me. And she hardly asked me, she told me that they were going to open a house for people with AIDS that night, Christmas Eve. She just didn't think about those things, for her there was no political advantage. She could have thought, "Well there might be some people who don't like the governor, that don't like the mayor, or some people who don't like me." She wanted to open a place for people with AIDS.

She was one of the first people in America who tried to do something for AIDS patients. Can you talk about her dedication, and the fact that she wanted no one to go to their deaths without knowing they were loved?

Yes, she never took any measures to protect herself. She would pick up babies with AIDS, or young men and old men, or young women and old women. She would hold them tight.

For her it was all-consuming, and if it became such for me, it was because of her. I had come to know a good bit about AIDS, professionally from textbooks. I had set myself to go to wash the bed pans or the sores of one thousand persons with AIDS. Talk to them and listen to them so that I would know something about them, that one tends to get caught up in trying to take care of the body there, one tends to get caught up in trying to bring some emotional fulfillment, that's a very good thing. Or to make this individual feel: nobody else wants you, but I want you.

But Mother Teresa always went right to the heart of the matter: You are a human being made in the image or likeness of God. You're probably going to die. I want to see that you get to heaven. For some that was a very simplistic approach, preaching to people who are very, very vulnerable. I never heard them accuse her of that, I saw many of them die with a happiness that would have been inconceivable for them otherwise. And I guess if you want to get at the essence of Mother Teresa it was always that. She always went to the heart of the matter.

She knew that there wasn't time to waste, and all sorts of people were telling them: You just hang on because there will be better drugs. You just hang on and show those people who don't understand, don't sympathize, the whole culture's going to change. As far as she was concerned this was a human soul in need of the divine touch, and she wasn't going to block that with any trivia.

Can you explain the special relationship Mother Teresa had with the Holy Father?

They are much alike in many ways. I have seen her with him, he treats her very deferentially. I remember we had a synod in Rome on consecrated life and Mother Teresa was there, and since I was assigned a particular responsibility at that time I had to meet the Holy Father every day and go with him to the synod hall, and back to his car, back to his own rooms. And every single day, virtually without exception, as we went down to his car, Mother Teresa would be standing nearby. Now there would be a hundred or so people standing there, but always he would signal to her to come over and it would be just a word.

Frequently she would tell him how many houses, or tabernacles as she would call them, she didn't speak of houses, how many sisters there are, little things, and always he would treat her with the greatest deference. She tried to genuflect, but he wouldn't let her. From my experience he has the same perspective, very direct. He's a virtual genius, theologically. He's a linguist, but he doesn't fool around. He goes straight to the heart of the matter, and when he's with you there's no one else in the world. You could be in a hall with ten thousand people, but he's talking to you. And he looks right into you as Mother Teresa would.

How should we remember Mother Teresa, and why is it important that we never forget her?

For each of us there is a personal input into not forgetting her. Certainly for me, every time I think "give God permission," every time I suggest this to someone, or talk about it publicly, the two are equated. So she's very important in that respect. For me to remember her simplicity is also very important.

The first time she ever came to the house we both sat on the couch and I said, "If I owned this house I would give it to you. But I'm only a prisoner here." And she said, "Well if you gave me this house, the first thing I would do if I owned this house would be to throw out those Oriental rugs onto the street." And I said, "Then you're not as smart as I thought you were, because you could sell these rugs for a bundle of money and give it to the poor." And we both laughed about it. Things like that I don't want to forget.

Obviously for the world at large to forget Mother Teresa is just to forget the poor, the sufferers, to forget the lepers, to forget the people with AIDS, and to forget God and that everyone is made in the image and likeness of his Son.

Mother Teresa did something which the pope always does—she treated *this* particular individual the same way precisely as she treated *that* individual. I have seen the Holy

Father meet presidents and royalty of every description, and I have seen him meet very simple people with very limited education of various religious persuasions, and he treats them all the same. So to forget Mother Teresa would be to risk forgetting the sacredness of every human person.

Give yourself fully to God. He will use you to accomplish great things on the condition that you believe much more in his love than in your own weakness.

MOTHER TERESA

That's the kind of person she was,
wholehearted and quick to act.

It is more than twenty-five years since I first met Mother
Teresa. I was a new bishop then, Cardinal Cooke's Vicar in the
Bronx and a pastor there. Mother Teresa's sisters had opened
a house for their work with the poor in the South Bronx, and
Mother was coming to visit them and ask how the work was
going. She had expressed a desire to see me, and so they invited me to meet her.

I must confess I felt somewhat intimidated, for her reputa-
tion as a saint was already well established and I was not sure
I quite knew how to act in the presence of a saint. I was afraid
she would size me up at a glance and decide I was not one, and
perhaps tell me so.

I was taken to an empty room in the convent, and there the
two of us met for the better part of an hour. The experience
was delightful and the conversation animated. If she was a
saint she seemed not in the least conscious of it, and she had
no interest at all in measuring my holiness. She was interested
only in the poor of the South Bronx and what she and her sisters might do to help them. She had the kindest eyes, and they

fairly danced for the love and the joy that was in them. I never met Mother Teresa again, except casually and briefly, but that first meeting will always remain a happy memory. It gave me the feeling that this woman was not only a saint but was one with whom it would be easy to work. No wonder she rallied so many to the side of the poor. In her frail little frame she carried the spirit of Jesus, and on her wrinkled face one could see his love.

When our meeting was over she asked if I would stay for breakfast. She ordered a fine one for me, and she sat and talked with me as I enjoyed it. She ate nothing herself, and I wondered whether she ever ate at all and was that why she was so thin. People came in and joined us, and soon the table was full. One of the visitors was Eileen Egan, who then was working for Catholic Relief Services, and had traveled the world to visit the poor, and to witness the work of Mother Teresa. She herself had just been down to Latin America and mentioned a country there where the poverty was worse than that in Calcutta. Mother reached into her pocketbook and pulled out a map. She handed it to Eileen and said, "Show me where that country is." When she pointed it out, Mother said to the sister who was traveling with her, "Get plane tickets for us. We'll go there before we return home." She went, and before long a mission of her Missionaries of Charity was established there. That's the kind of person she was, wholehearted and quick to act to relieve the sufferings of the poor and let them feel the love of God for them.

She will be greatly missed. From heaven she will help us with her prayers, and her amazing sisters will carry on her work for years and years to come.

Just allow people to see Jesus in you.

MOTHER TERESA

GENE PRINCIPE

VOLUNTEER, NEW YORK

Gene Principe is one of Mother Teresa's most devoted volunteers. He remembers when her home for AIDS patients opened in New York, and the profound effect it had on the last days of one man's life.

We first opened the *Gift of Love* in New York, the home for AIDS patients, on Christmas Eve 1985, and Mother had gone up to Sing-Sing prison to bring three men down with her. Only one was able to move in that night, and I had the privilege to spend the evening with him when the sisters and other volunteers had gone to Christmas Eve Mass. His name was Ramon Galvin. Five days later he died, but he died with dignity, concern, and care because of Mother Teresa.

> *I see God in every human being. When I wash the leper's wounds, I feel I am nursing the Lord himself.*
> *Is it not a beautiful experience?*
>
> MOTHER TERESA

JOSEPH MATOS MORALES

AIDS PATIENT, NEW YORK

My faith has been restored.

It was back in January 1998, a few months after Mother Teresa's death, that I was given a miraculous medal that had been blessed by her. My own mother was a practicing Roman Catholic and a New York City school teacher. She died on September 6, 1996.

I was diagnosed with AIDS in March 1994; my t-cells were at ninety. Over the past twenty months they have climbed as high as 236.

For the past thirty years I was a homosexual, but since I got my medal my faith has been restored and I have taken a vow of chastity in honor of Saint Joseph, my confirmation name.

On September 6, 1998, the second anniversary of my mother's death, I started to read *The Catholic Truths*, a book about illustrious saints containing teachings of the holy Catholic church. I then embarked on a decision of going back to the Catholic church and confessing myself to a priest so as to be able to receive holy communion once again. My days of living as a pagan were over with; at last a final battle with my soul had come to pass.

Over the next two weeks I struggled with my conscience. How would I confess thirty years of sins? I found myself in between my body and my soul, particularly knowing that my mother had made great sacrifices as a single working mother to send me to Catholic grammar school. Finally, after two weeks, I took a walk to the Catholic church near my house and walked in.

There on the altar was a tall slender priest who was marrying a Filipino couple. I sat at the back of the church and listened to the priest speak about having been a professional basketball player in the Philippines for five years. What struck me about him was his Christ-like appearance, and I could see in him the capacity to understand and help.

I said to God, "Oh Lord, if only I could know what his name is and when he was hearing confession." But the wedding finished and I went and stood outside the church. I watched the happy and blessed couple leave for their honeymoon, thinking about my own parents' wedding. I left feeling sad and walked over to the rectory. I found out that between 4:00 and 5:30 that afternoon there would be confessions.

I dragged myself to church and sat down on the pew. I saw one priest walk in, saw another, but not the basketball player. Forty minutes had passed and I was nervous and sweating and had thoughts about leaving. Then all of a sudden I turned around to go out of the church and one of the confessional lights was lit, but I had not seen the priest who went in there.

I held my breath and opened the door and by God's divine grace it was the priest basketball player. He confessed me in a grueling two-hour-confession with sobs and tears. I told him about the Mother Teresa medal, and he was truly concerned about my soul. The next day I went to Mass and took holy communion. Time passed and I kept going to church on Sundays, always confessing myself on Saturday.

Since receiving the miraculous medal that was blessed by Mother Teresa, my life has been transformed spiritually in a way beyond anything I ever thought was possible.

The most important thing to do to change my heart is confession. After confession, holy communion.

MOTHER TERESA

First lady Hillary Rodham Clinton meets with Mother Teresa at the opening of the Mother Teresa Home for Infant Children in 1995, in Washington.

As soon as your eyes locked onto hers, as soon as she took your hand in hers, you knew you were in the presence of an extraordinary and exceptional human being.

She was attending the National Prayer Breakfast which presidents have always attended since the 1950s. Mother Teresa was the annual speaker in February 1994. She had sent word that she wanted to meet privately with my husband and me. So after the breakfast was over, we went into a little room, behind the curtains of the large ballroom, and she said she had something she wanted to talk to me about. We sat and Mother Teresa took my hands and she began to talk to me about her desire to have a home for infants and children here in Washington, D.C.

In her direct and persuasive way she said, "Now will you help me?"

And I said, "Of course I will help you." So my first meeting with her was not only memorable, of course, but also typical, because when Mother Teresa met people of all walks of life—but certainly, the political life—she always had a mission for them. That was the mission she gave to me.

Everyone who knew her would account that she was a very thin but powerful presence. Physically she was not at all tall or imposing, and years and years of hard work on behalf of the poor and the destitute and ill had caused her to become more bent over. She did not really convey any sense of immediate greatness across the room. But as soon as she came into your presence, as soon as your eyes locked onto hers, as soon as she took your hand in hers, you knew you were in the presence of an extraordinary and exceptional human being. And she had an extraordinary sense of humor. She was blunt, but with a kind smile about her bluntness.

She was a woman of great strength, extraordinary presence of great personal strength and courage, but really the word great is the most applicable to what she conveyed and how she did the work.

She falls for me in a very special category of people who have a spiritual presence about them. I have met many powerful, famous, rich, and accomplished people, and there's an excitement, an energy, a charisma certainly around many of them. But with Mother Teresa you really felt she was clearly demonstrating what it meant to be a servant of God, that in your presence with her something happened, that the energy that was created was more than the sum of the parts. I always felt around her, and watching her, that she just conveyed this extraordinarily strong sense of what it meant to be a person of faith. What it meant to live out the golden rule to love and care for each other. It wasn't about her, like it is with so many celebrities.

Mother Teresa used her faith to reach out to people of all religions, who needed a message of love, caring, and hope. She did it at a time when it is very easy for us who inhabit this rich, affluent, global economy to turn a blind eye to the cries of the poorest of the poor. Because she was willing to show us where they lived, where they suffered, what they needed, we can never walk away again. Mother Teresa left us with a tremendous legacy. That should be a challenge to the rest of us.

I'm just a little pencil in his hand. Tomorrow, if he finds somebody more helpless, more hopeless, I think he will do still greater things with her and through her.

MOTHER TERESA

KEVIN McMAHON

BUSINESSMAN, NEW YORK

Words cannot express how profoundly touched we have been.

This story is a compelling and beautiful account of how Mother Teresa forever changed his family's life.

On December 7, 1995, I was rushing to LaGuardia Airport to catch a shuttle flight to Boston. I worked for an investment bank, C.S. First Boston, and was on my way to a charity dinner called "The Cotting School Party," which is one of the best of the Christmas season charity events, both in terms of spirit and funds raised. At approximately 3:00 p.m. I was sprinting through the airport to make a flight. I looked over to my right and saw a sight that was very different from the usual banality and humdrum of airport scenes. Squatting and kneeling on the ground was a group of about ten nuns surrounding a much older sister. She was speaking to them and they were completely zeroed in on her words, ignoring the rush of businessmen around them. I remember thinking how young the sisters all looked, and reflected on the old adage that when policemen began to look like children, you know you're growing old.

Since I had just turned thirty-eight, I hoped it didn't apply to sisters also. Then I stopped suddenly in my tracks as I realized the older one speaking looked just like Mother Teresa. I shyly moved over near the spot, not wanting to interrupt their moment. Mother was telling the girls that we all have to do more, that America's problems are spiritual and deep. One of the sisters asked Mother if she could come back for her birthday, a request that drew a few giggles from the nuns as well as a few of the onlookers. Mother gently told her she would try. It dawned on me that I was going to miss my flight, but I decided to let it go to watch this. A few other travelers did the same.

Mother explained to her little community on the rug that she had to leave now to go to Washington. She gave them a final blessing and said she had a gift for them and handed them each a miraculous medal. She slowly but gracefully got up to depart, and it was as if all the airport, including the airport workers, had stopped still. She saw me standing there, probably gawking, and she motioned to what appeared to be one of the local convent community to go over to me.

The sister came over and said, "Mother wants you to have a miraculous medal." I eagerly accepted. Then she asked me if I was married. When I nodded yes, she said to give one to my wife and to tell her it had been blessed by Mother. She then asked me if I had any children. I said no, that we had been hoping for quite some time. The sister placed a third medal in my hand and spoke what would later prove to be a prophetic phrase: "This medal is for the child we will pray God sends you very soon." Then she excused herself and went back to Mother, who smiled at me as she was making her way toward a gate. The other nuns made preparations to return to a van they had outside.

Upon boarding the next flight, I took the in-flight credit-card phone out and went through the age-old quandary every Irishman has after encountering the event of a lifetime: Do I call Mom first or my wife first? Mom loved the story and cried a bit. An hour later at the benefit, I showed off my medals and told everyone who would listen my story. Richard McDonald, who along with Kay McDonough is one of the organizers, had a classic response: "Kevin, if you were a real salesman, you would have talked Mother Teresa into coming to our benefit here tonight!"

As 1996 came I often thought of the event, especially since winter and spring came and went with still no gift of a child. In late summer my brother Patrick came to my wife Lisa and me with a situation he had heard of from his friends at a crisis pregnancy center. An Irish nanny living in New York was pregnant and had an abortion scheduled. She had decided to see if there was a cheaper price available and accidentally called the pregnancy center. They explained to her that they didn't do abortions, but they would give her a free pregnancy test and tell her about other options. She had the courage to go and was shown the tape *Eclipse of Reason* and was befriended by one of the counselors, a registered nurse. The counselor and girl scheduled a dinner for two days hence. She said she would consider adoption but would want a good doctor, lawyer, hospital, and a job. She pointedly summed up her predicament by stating "Who would hire a pregnant nanny? That's why I have to abort." The test showed she was five months along.

Lisa and I, after much fearful discussion, made the decision to get involved and get her the things she needed. Two days later, she chose life and adoption for her child. As I'm told often happens in "saves and turnarounds," the young lady enjoyed an easy pregnancy. On December 6 she bore a baby girl after a quick labor in a hospital in New Jersey. On December 7, 1996, just after 3:00 p.m., Lisa and I were handed Julia Mary in the hospital lobby. It was one year, almost to the minute, from when I had been given the miraculous medal by Mother and her assistant.

Words cannot express how profoundly touched we have been by these agents of the Lord, the nuns, the pregnancy counselors, Julia's biological mother, and Mother Teresa herself.

> *The best and surest way to learn the love of Jesus is through the family.*
>
> MOTHER TERESA

SENATOR   EDWARD   KENNEDY

WASHINGTON,   D.C.

I'm most grateful to you
for [your] continuing inspiration.

*In August 1995 Senator Kennedy wrote a letter to Mother
Teresa and enclosed a copy of Rose Fitzgerald Kennedy's
book* Times to Remember. *Senator Kennedy said the following in the letter:*

I'm most grateful to you for the continuing inspiration that
your faith and good works and example have been to me in
my life and in my work in the United States Senate on behalf
of children and the poor.

In my own family, my mother, who passed away earlier this
year, was a lifelong example to all of us for her own remarkable faith. I thought you might like to have the enclosed copy
of the book which she wrote many years ago, and which was
reissued this year. Near the end of her book, on page 444, she
expressed the philosophy that she lived by—"If God were to
take away all his blessings, health, physical fitness, wealth,
intelligence, and leave me but one gift, I would ask for faith."

I know that my mother, too, was truly inspired by your
extraordinary life and faith.

Senator Kennedy's inscription in the book was:

```
To Mother Teresa,

whose faith and ideals and example have
inspired all the Kennedys,

With respect and admiration,

Edward M. Kennedy
```

On September 8, 1997, after the death of Mother Teresa, Senator Kennedy went to the Embassy of India in Washington and signed the book of condolences for Mother Teresa with the following inscription:

Our hearts go out to the people of India on the loss of Mother Teresa. Her extraordinary life and faith made the world a better place for all those who need our help the most. May her life and legacy inspire people and governments in every land to carry on her work, which is truly God's work on earth.

Love has to be put into action, and that action is service.

MOTHER TERESA

ISMAIL MERCHANT

INDIAN FILMMAKER

Mother Teresa was the mother to all of India.

Mother Teresa's name for India evokes humanity . . . an intensely selfless human being who devoted her life to uplifting human beings, not just in India but all over the world.

Mother Teresa did something that touched the whole world.

A person like Mother Teresa, who did not have any money, did something that shook the whole world and made a tremendous difference to the people in India and all over the world, and that I think is important.

Other well-known people have a temporary status. Mother Teresa has what you can call permanent status, not only in this world, but in the world of the future. What Mother Teresa stood for is a much greater accomplishment than that of show-business people. They come and go, but Mother Teresa's work is so profound and so accomplished that it will be remembered for all time.

Celebrities have a lot to learn from Mother Teresa. If you take the life of a celebrity, it is a very empty life. If you [look for] someone who has devoted their time and energy to our civilization, there are very few in show business. But Mother Teresa has. She inspired us. Mother did it without motive, and that is why we admire her so much.

To my country of India she brought hope to the lives of millions of people. She gave them homes, she gave them help, she cured them. These people were deprived of family and alone, and she brought that to them. You could see people with disease, who were hated people, and they got a lift in their life. She brought smiles to so many people.

Mother Teresa was the mother to all of India; that is the highest compliment one can give her. I think the work that she started has such a strong foundation to it that it will continue forever.

I will work all day. That is the best way.

MOTHER TERESA

FR. RAVAVEITINU

INDIAN PRIEST

Mother Teresa . . . made you feel special, very special.

*I*n my opinion, Mother Teresa was a bright light shining in the darkness. She was the one who took the poor out of the dark. That was a great thing for India and a great show of love.

When I met her for the first time in 1971, Mother Teresa was tied to Calcutta. I cannot think of Calcutta without Mother Teresa—she is the whole city. The difference between Mother Teresa and other people is the love. She used to tell me she loved the poor people and we work for the poorest of the poor. And I can never forget those words. She took the poorest of the poor in her heart, and that is what distinguished her from other saints. She was a special saint of the poorest of the poor.

I told her once, "You are called to be a saint," and she said we are all called to be saints. I thought that was cute. It was thoughtful for her to answer that way.

The difference, in my opinion, between Mother Teresa and other celebrities is that when you are in front of them you know they are special, and when you were with Mother Teresa she made you feel special, very special.

Mother made everyone feel great.

Intense love does not measure; it just gives.

MOTHER TERESA

I think Mother Teresa is still a light, an inspiration . . . a hope.

I think Diana would love to be here to talk about their friendship, and I cannot answer for her, but I do know that Mother Teresa was like a mother figure and together they were wonderful humanitarians. I think that all of her life Diana loved that feeling of an older person. I think she saw Mother Teresa as a wonderful person in her soul. Diana was an extraordinary humanitarian and she looked to Mother Teresa for advice on the best way to go forward. When Diana died, there was a feeling that we must keep going, we must go forward. There wasn't anyone with a better sense of humor than Diana. And when Mother Teresa died with all her devotion, it is important to keep these feelings inside of us. Both deaths were such a difficult time for us, but let's get on with these feelings in our life.

Years from now, how would I describe Mother Teresa?

I would describe Mother Teresa as an extraordinary prophet, like a saint, a woman who stood up with devotion and passion, a real genuine woman, who stood up for her beliefs with courage and devotion. All those good words are lost in our world at the moment, which is a world of madness, running around in a rat race. I think it's time that we all looked in our hearts to the love that Mother Teresa exuded to everyone. I remember Mother Teresa used to say that "The greatest disease of all is the lack of love in the world," and I think, "What greater saying can you have in your mind on a daily basis than to come from your heart and your mind with deep love?"

I think Mother Teresa is still a light, an inspiration, a hope . . . beyond everything. She was a lady that was willing to put everything aside and give from her heart.

She was this fragile little light, and I think people are frightened by the light. People want to know what it is about this little woman. Why does she have this amazing desire to help others? People may be frightened by it. But actually Mother Teresa was just this wonderful, small, little shining star that shone all over the world to get groups of people together.

To keep a lamp burning we have to keep putting oil in it.

MOTHER TERESA

HIS ROYAL HIGHNESS PRINCE PHILIP

BUCKINGHAM PALACE, ENGLAND

---

*Mother Teresa has shown by her life what people
can do when their faith is strong.*

*His Royal Highness Prince Philip suggested I include his
speech made on April 23, 1973, when Mother Teresa was
presented with the Templeton Prize.*

At first sight the idea that a prize might be able to do something for religion seems faintly absurd. A prize, in the ordinary sense, is an encouragement to succeed or recognition of some measurable achievement. A prize is usually something to be striven for.

In the case of a prize for religion, the only certainty is that those who are worthy to receive it will most definitely not have striven for it. I simply cannot conceive the possibility of anyone coldly deciding to do something for religion in order to win this prize. In any case, is it really possible for even the most worthy and distinguished judges to decide whether one person has done God's work better than another? I frankly admit that I was very much in two minds about this idea, even though I realized perfectly well that Mr. Templeton had not conceived this as a prize in the conventional sense.

I respected the intention of his imaginative proposal and I have every confidence in the judges, but I doubted whether it would work.

Then came the news of the person selected to receive the prize, together with a description of Mother Teresa's work, particularly among the very poor in Calcutta. I am sure Mr. Templeton will forgive me for saying so, but it is really Mother Teresa who has made this prize work in the way it was intended.

The usual procedure on these occasions is to congratulate the prize winner. I don't think there is any question of doing that today. In this case, we can only be thankful for Mother Teresa's work and grateful to the judges for drawing our attention to it. It is Mr. Templeton and the judges who are to be congratulated for having Mother Teresa accept the Templeton prize.

I have already said that I had misgivings about this idea. The misgivings have gone and I freely admit that my first reactions were wrong. However, they have been replaced by even greater misgivings about what I am supposed to be doing here. The sheer goodness which shines through Mother Teresa's life and work can only inspire humility.

There is nothing I can say about Mother Teresa, but I think there is much to be learned from her example. I believe that the lesson which we should learn from this occasion is a very simple one and a very old one. It is just that the strength of a person's faith is measured by his actions. St. Paul puts it this way, "What is it for a man to say he has faith when he does nothing to show it?" Mother Teresa would not have done it without an overpowering faith.

Indeed I do not believe there is any other way of measuring faith except through daily actions and behavior. No ceremonies, no protestations, no displays, no routines of prayer, and no theorizing can compare with the smallest act of genuine and practical compassion as a true reflection of personal faith.

I think there is a very natural tendency for many people to look upon God as the all-powerful creator and then to work downwards looking for his influence on events and for his continuing control of the world. I suspect that it might be better to begin with the evidence of the lives of people like Mother Teresa—that is if there is anyone else quite like her—and to work with that evidence towards a better understanding of the power of God. Their work and achievements are really beyond what can reasonably be expected from members of the genus Homo in the strictly biological scientific sense.

Yet they are ordinary flesh and blood; the difference is their motivation, their inspiration, the driving force within them. The nature of that force can be seen quite clearly in the works which it inspires, and if it is capable of so transforming an individual it must be very powerful indeed. It is in the lives of such people that the nature and influence of God is to be recognized, and it is there that it should be expected, and not in some inconsistent intervention in the process of the mechanism of nature.

A tremendous power has entered into Mother Teresa. It might, of course, have found her anyway. But I suspect that she was moved to seek this power of God and it was able to reach her because she was brought up within the Christian tradition. It was through the influence of a devout family and community that she became aware of the idea of God as loving and compassionate. It was this introduction which opened up the line of communication and made it possible for the message to reach her. I hope that her example and her Order in their turn may be the means by which the Christian idea is made alive and apparent to a great many people.

Not everyone exposed to the Christian tradition is going to get a message quite in this way, but the chances of getting any useful message at all without some experience of a religious environment and without any will to serve God is very small indeed. The idea that the world can easily do without religious inspiration betrays a very limited outlook. The extent to which humanity had been converted from groups of superior animals to peaceful and compassionate communities is largely due to the vision and to the example of the great religious leaders.

If that process towards more civilized living is to go on, many more people will have to be exposed to religious thought, so that some at least can open up a line of communication which may eventually allow a message to get through. Those who receive a message, whether weak or strong, will have to live and work by it every moment of their lives.

Without the chance of receiving the message, the most well-meaning, energetic, and intelligent human being is really no more than a bumblebee trapped in a bottle. Without the sort of moral inspiration which is the whole purpose of religion, all our institutions become rather pointless. Why bother to educate? Is it possible to have a purposeless culture? What is the point of justice? Why be concerned about the weak and the helpless, isn't honesty just a vain hope?

Mother Teresa has shown by her life what people can do when the faith is strong. By any standards what she has done is good. The world today is desperately in need of this sort of goodness, this sort of practical compassion. I hope this prize will help Mother Teresa in her work, but I also hope that everyone who hears about this event and perhaps as a result of it learns a little about the life and work of Mother Teresa, will gain a better understanding of what is meant by faith.

It gives me the very greatest pleasure to present the Templeton Prize to Mother Teresa.

*H*er Royal Highness Princess Caroline feels tremendous respect and admiration for Mother Teresa whose entire life was pledged and committed to the poorest people.

The trouble is that rich people, well-to-do people, very often don't really know who the poor are; and that is why we can forgive them, for knowledge can only lead to love, and love to service. And so, if they are not touched by them, it's because they do not know them.

MOTHER TERESA

ORPHANED IN CALCUTTA

I'm alive and it's because of Mother Teresa.

Susan Van Haute, once an orphan in Calcutta, is now a mother and happily married woman, living twenty-nine years later in Boston, Massachusetts.

Mother Teresa saved my life. I'm living proof of her good works.

I was born thirty years ago in Calcutta. I figured that my own mother was too poor to have me, and she probably went off and died somewhere. But she was smart enough to go to Mother Teresa's home, and she went to Mother and asked her to look after me. And I am here today because of the grace of God and Mother Teresa, and it's a miracle. I am more than happy to tell the world what she has done. I'm alive and it's because of Mother Teresa. I could have died on the streets of Calcutta, and instead I'm alive because she takes people off the streets and brings them back to life. I am more than happy to tell the world about what she has done because it's a miracle—truly a miracle. I was frail and sickly and I wouldn't have survived on Calcutta's filthy streets. Three months later I was adopted by an American woman and her husband, a British doctor. We moved to America, and when I was twelve years old they told me about the adoption. They explained who Mother Teresa was and about her dedication to the poor.

In 1995 Mother Teresa came to Boston and we sat together for nearly an hour and I thanked Mother for saving my life. As we talked, Mother squeezed my hand and I felt as if I was looking into the eyes of a saint. Mother blessed my family and we prayed together. Then she invited me to come to Calcutta and spend a few weeks as a volunteer at her mission. She told me, "It's not how much we give but how much we put into the giving."

I owe my life to Mother Teresa. That's a debt I can never repay, but I will try.

It's not how much we give but how much we put into the giving.

MOTHER TERESA

GERALD HERBERT

PHOTOGRAPHER

On the streets of Calcutta there are families, mothers, children, and corpses. It is quite profound.

I think it gave me a sense of peace seeing the exchange of love that Mother Teresa and her sisters gave to the poor, and I realized my life wasn't so bad.

AGNES MAITY

CALCUTTA GRANDMOTHER

Agnes Maity is a fifty-six-year-old grandmother. She was a child of eight in the Motijil slums in suburban Calcutta when she first met Mother Teresa.

I was a girl when Mother picked me up in her arms. She got my brothers into good schools and got them good jobs. She always intervened. This area was saved only because of Mother. Who will take care of us now?

BRITAN CANTOPHER

CALCUTTA

Britan Cantopher lives across the street from the mother-house, the Missionaries of Charity's headquarters in Calcutta.

I've watched her come to the door, pay the taxi, and take in a woman whose husband threw her out because she was pregnant with a girl. I've seen her pick up unwanted children left on her doorstep, and lepers who came to her house.

SUVIR SARAN

NEW DELHI

She took the sari, a Hindu costume, and adapted it to work for her order. She could have taken a religious habit, but she knew she had to be one of the people to help the people. The people of India loved her. For us she was our saint.

BIMA NATH

CALCUTTA, INDIA

I no longer drink.

Bima has only a blurred memory of the first time he saw Mother Teresa. His wife had left him because he used to beat her up when he was drunk. Mother Teresa's sisters picked him up, believing him to be sick and homeless, and took him to one of Mother's shelters, where he spent the night in a drunken stupor, and woke up to find her inspecting the home.

The other people in the home said she was a saint. They said they were treated like animals until they met her. I am a municipal street sweeper and most people avoid us because the work is dirty, we look filthy and smell. But she used to touch us and never bothered about how we looked. Since I was healthier than the others, Mother Teresa asked me to help out with the work in the shelter. My wife had left me because I used to beat her when I was drunk.

There was a lot of cleaning to be done. She also kept an eye on my drinking. She never shouted at me when I took to drink, but the look of disappointment on her face upset me. I realize now that she was testing me to see if I could handle another job or if drinking had ruined my life. I no longer drink. I owe my job to her since it was Mother who told me to apply for work with the local civic authorities.

> *If you are really in love with Christ, no matter how small your work, it will be done better; it will be wholehearted.*
>
> MOTHER TERESA

CAROLINE COLLYMORE
FLIGHT ATTENDANT

I have met a lot of people as a flight attendant. Mother Teresa was just such a spiritual person, she was just about helping other people. When she was on the flight, the whole experience was very special.

LINDA GRANT
FIRST CLASS LOUNGE, KENNEDY AIRPORT

*I*n my humble opinion there is no one like Mother Teresa. I have seen dignitaries, princes, and people from all walks of life here at Kennedy airport. If Mother Teresa was here at the airport, I have seen them get down on their knees and ask for a blessing. You have no idea what people would become in the face of this tiny little woman.

A TEENAGER

She's not famous because of the way that she danced or what she wore but because of her tremendous deeds. And she did countless of them, just helping other people.

FRED SCHWARTZ

AIDS VOLUNTEER

Because of Mother I have been all over the world teaching people about AIDS.

> *The world today is hungry not only for bread but hungry for love; hungry to be wanted, to be loved.*
>
> MOTHER TERESA

FR. ANDREW GREELEY

CHICAGO PRIEST

Talking to Mother was like a week-long retreat.

Saints, real saints, are magical. They are luminous, transparent, irresistible.

They enchant, enthrall us, captivate us. They seem to be qualitatively different from the rest of humankind. They attract us not by preaching, much less by screeching, but by radiant goodness, irrepressible cheerfulness, and devastating love. We are compelled to follow them, not because of what they say, but because of who they are. Our aim is not necessarily to do what they do, but rather, to try to be what they are.

So I discovered one hot June afternoon during the late 1960s in southern Ohio as I rode in a cab for an hour with Mother Teresa. I entered the cab drained, after a lecture in a stuffy auditorium, and cynical about the misguided enthusiasm that was the Catholic fashion in those days. I left the cab renewed, energized, happy. Talking to Mother was like a week-long retreat.

The subjects discussed were not important. We could have talked about the Chicago Cubs and her effect on me would have been the same. For that hour ride I was in the presence of goodness, the likes of which I had never encountered before, one that opened up new horizons of possibility in my life. I knew that I could never be as good as Mother Teresa, but that I could be better than I was. I could be almost as radiantly happy as she was. That is the most vivid of my memories of one hour, she was the happiest human being I had ever met.

This is the true reason for our existence, to be the sunshine of God's love.

MOTHER TERESA

FR. JOSEPH F. WIMMER, O.S.A.

WASHINGTON, D.C.

I took her advice to heart and am still an Augustinian.

Father Joseph has two stories about Mother Teresa's infinite wisdom.

I met Mother Teresa in Rome in 1972. I was teaching Old Testament to her novices at Torre del Fiscale, and when Mother arrived there I asked her to give a talk to our Augustinian seminarians in Rome. She graciously did so. Sometime later, I told her I was busy writing my doctoral dissertation (at the Gregorian University), but was not making much progress. Perhaps God was calling me to leave the Augustinians and join the Missionaries of Charity. She told me that when someone applied to the Missionaries of Charity from another religious congregation, she required that they leave their former congregation for at least one year, and only then apply to the Missionaries of Charity if they still felt the calling. Furthermore, before they leave, they should live perfectly according to the rules and constitutions of their own congregation. I took her advice to heart, and am still an Augustinian. I finished the dissertation, and am now teaching in a Catholic school of theology, the Washington Theological Union, Washington, D.C.

On one occasion in Rome, in the mid-seventies, a convent of Augustinian contemplative nuns (at Saint Quattro Coronati) asked me to bring Mother Teresa to see them, since they were unable to leave their convent to see her. Mother Teresa agreed, and had a beautiful visit with them. Many of the nuns were crying with joy and admiration, and a number of them got Mother Teresa to autograph their holy cards. At the end of the visit the superior of the convent, Madre Alessandra, asked Mother Teresa if there was anything she needed, something they could do for her. Mother said that she had many novices at Torre del Fiscale, so many, in fact, that some sisters had no beds to sleep on. They were using doors as beds. She needed more beds.

I thought to myself, what an odd request. How can contemplative nuns get extra beds? But to my surprise, Madre Alessandra said she would be glad to help, since she was a friend of the Italian Minister of the Interior. She had but to call him, and he would supply the beds. A week later so many beds were delivered to Mother Teresa's sisters by the Italian government that they had to give some of the beds away.

> *Like Jesus we belong to the world, living not for ourselves but for others. The joy of the Lord is our strength.*
>
> MOTHER TERESA

Mother Teresa had a major influence on my life.

She would say to me, "Never, ever get discouraged. If there are a hundred people in great need, then help one and maybe you can help more than one. Maybe you can help ten or twenty and then maybe you can help the full hundred. Because at the end of the day it's not your work anyway. It is God's work and you're just a weak instrument in his hands."

On this road of life, I've met some wonderful people who helped me enormously. Mother Teresa of Calcutta, whom I met for the first time in Ethiopia in 1973, had a major influence on my life. It is difficult to imitate her, but I tried. She had a great simplicity, dynamic faith, unlimited generosity, kindness, transparent goodness, and genuine charity. I was privileged to work closely with her for more than twenty years, and have seen her influence on so many people in Africa, Europe, and the Middle East. A woman for all seasons, she appealed to the young and the elderly, of every race and color. Mother Teresa put hundreds, even thousands, of young volunteers through her hands. She registered them in Calcutta. She loved them and they loved her. Many will tell you that their time working for Mother Teresa was the highlight of their lives. I have seen them at Mass at 6:30 a.m. in the motherhouse of the Missionaries of Charity, in Lower Circular Road in Calcutta. Many have rediscovered their faith in the slums of Calcutta, or nursing a dying person in Kaligat Temple, run by Mother Teresa's sisters, rather than listening to a sermon in church, however eloquent.

Mother Teresa drew good out of everything and everybody. I once visited Calcutta shortly after she had fallen ill, and was struck by the strong reactions of the people to her illness. One wealthy Muslim left his work and did a pilgrimage to Mecca so that God would not take her away. A Hindu boy wrote directly to God: "Dear God, please do not take our Mother away from us." The local paper carried a cartoon depicting the churches' reaction to her sickness. It showed a mosque, a Hindu temple, a Buddhist temple, and a Christian church. Outside each building, members of each congregation stood dressed in their respective costumes, with their hands joined together in prayer as they looked up to heaven. The caption underneath was: "O God, please do not take our Mother away from us." The cartoon clearly illustrated the respect and acceptance that everyone in the world had for Mother Teresa.

Irrespective of nationality, creed, or color, Mother Teresa's prayer life stands out as an example to all. She attributed all her success to God's loving intervention. She attributed nothing to herself. God used her as an instrument of his divine power, and there is no one to compare with her today—so weak-looking and yet so strong, so frail and yet so dynamic. Her death has deprived the world of a shining light in the darkness.

Never, ever get discouraged.

MOTHER TERESA

Amanda Mays, 20, poses in Portland, Oregon, 1997, with a copy of Newsweek showing the 1978 image taken by photographer Eddie Adams of Mother Teresa holding Mays as a baby.

Mother is my guardian angel.

Amanda was born without arms in Calcutta. She now lives in America thanks to Mother Teresa.

Mother Teresa rescued me when I was just eight months old and took me away from a life where I was destined to die. She found me crying and alone in an orphan crib in the orphanage, but seeing me without arms in those conditions she knew I was destined to die. And so she arranged for me to be adopted, and to be brought to America.

I don't complain about being born without arms twenty-one years ago, it's something that I've had to deal with. Even now I see Mother Teresa's kindly face in my dreams, and I am bathed over with happiness. I believe Mother is my guardian angel. Mother Teresa taught us that as human beings, it is our mission to be responsible for each other.

Yesterday is gone. Tomorrow has not yet come.
We have only today. Let us begin.

MOTHER TERESA

in memoriam

Mother Teresa releases a dove for peace at a 1982 rally of 20,000 people for Youth Corporation in Toronto.

Born August 26, 1910

Died September 5, 1997

I choose the poverty of our poor people. But I am grateful to receive [the Nobel] in the name of the hungry, the naked, the homeless, of the crippled, of the blind, of the lepers, of all those people who feel unwanted, unloved, uncared-for throughout society, people that have become a burden to the society and are shunned by everyone.

FROM THE NOBEL PEACE PRIZE ACCEPTANCE SPEECH

*W*hen you have Christ, you are rich, and he is sufficient for you: he will provide for you, and will be your faithful procurator in all things.

THE IMITATION OF CHRIST

PRAYER FOR MOTHER TERESA

(APPROVED FOR PRIVATE USE BY THE ARCHBISHOP OF CALCUTTA)

*G*od our loving Father,

You have exalted the beauty of your love for us in the life of Mother Teresa of Calcutta.

She showed the poor and the suffering, the weak and the lonely how much you long to love them—how in their poverty and pain you thirst for them through Jesus your Son. It was he, hidden in the poor, whom she served as her Lord and loved as her Spouse.

May her example encourage us to recognize Jesus in our brothers and sisters in need and reach out to them with ardor and joy, kindness and compassion, as she did.

May her work here continue and we ask you, Dear Father, that through her intercession your grace will touch our weakness and heal our wounds.

We ask this special favor through the intercession of your handmaid, Mother Teresa.

(MENTION THE SPECIAL FAVOR PRAYED FOR.)

May the beauty of her life, holiness, and message be lifted up by the Church, even as she lifted the beauty of your Son's presence in the precious disguise of the poor.

AMEN

> *Mother Teresa did it for Jesus.*
>
> *Let us now pray to him for her.*

Acclaimed author SUSAN CRIMP has written six books, including *Iron Rose: A Biography of Rose Fitzgerald Kennedy* and *Caroline and Stephanie* about Monaco's royal family. Also a journalist and television producer, Crimp has been commended by several humanitarian organizations for her reporting on international disasters. Save the Children honored her "selfless efforts . . . to make lasting and positive differences in the lives of disadvantaged children." A documentary film about Mother Teresa that Crimp is producing and directing inspired *Touch by a Saint*. "The memory of this remarkable woman," Crimp says, "needs to be preserved for all time." Crimp lives in New York City.